Make Your Business Sizzle

12 Tactics You May Never Learn Anywhere Else

Written by
Gene LaNier

"The test of a first-rate intelligence is the ability to hold two opposed ideas in mind at the same time and still retain the ability to function. "

- F. Scott Fitzgerald

About the author

Mr. LaNier is a native of North Carolina and a graduate of The University of North Carolina at Chapel Hill. He continued his education with postgraduate studies at New York University, and the University of Central Florida.

For eleven years, Mr. LaNier served as an adjunct professor for Public Relations, Marketing and Advertising courses at the main campus of Daytona State College in Daytona Beach, Florida. He also served on the school's business advisory board.

He is listed in Who's Who in Public Relations, sixth edition, 1992. He was named one of the "world's top public relations professionals" in the book, The Pro Challenge, 1994.

He received accreditation from the Public Relations Society of America in 1976 and was a member of the Society's Counselors Academy. He has been a member of the American Marketing Association, the Florida Public Relations Association, The American Advertising Federation, The National Association of Real Estate Editors and the German-based Visit USA Committee.

He is a previous member of The World Future Society, The Society for Scholarly Publishing and the International Association of Business Communicators.

Mr. LaNier has won numerous national and international awards for advertising and public relations excellence. He has authored several articles for trade and consumer publications. He has been a featured speaker at conferences and seminars throughout the United States, Canada and parts of Europe.

Mr. LaNier worked in the Marketing, Advertising and Public Relations fields for several major corporations including Manufacturers Life Insurance Company of Canada, General Development Corporation in Miami and ITT Corp of New York, The rest of his career has been on the agency and consulting side.

Contents

Introduction

Tough times never last, tough people do. Dr. Robert Schuler used those words as a title of one of his best sellers. The statement says it all. We all have been through tough times. Life is cyclical. Good times roll around and then bad ones come again. But we can be tougher than anything life throws at us. It's all about attitude.

Everyone in the world faces tough times and tough problems. It's how we handle those tough times and tough problems that makes the difference in our lives. That difference can be an opportunity for a miracle or a catastrophe. It is totally up to each of us.

In this book are some strategies to help you build and strengthen your business in good times and bad. These are practical applications of marketing principles. They work just as a wrench of the correct size will work to tighten a bolt.

These pages can help lift you out of mediocrity and put you into a success mode that will help you earn more money and gain more financial freedom that you ever dreamed possible. You will discover the only thing standing in your way to success is you.

Foreword

What is the first thing you do when you walk into a room filled with people? If you are like most people, the first thing you do is look around, find out what's happening, who's there. Then, you decide your next step.

It is the same procedure when you start a business or add a new customer. You want to look around. Ask many questions. Listen. When starting or taking over a business, one of the most obvious things you want to discover is how much competition exists and how well entrenched competitors are. Are they direct competitors or indirect? Are their prices the same as yours? Almost the same? Cheaper?

It does not hurt to visit with people you will consider as prospects when you open. Learn how the market functions. Is it difficult to make a buck or is it a well-developed market with plenty for all? A large county in Florida appears to have a healthy business climate, but a closer look tells a different story.

In fact, the local business joke is, " How do you become a millionaire in this county?" The answer is, "Bring two when you come." If possible, compare the market today with twenty years ago to determine progress or the lack of it. Is a good old boy system in control?

Large corporations spend small fortunes investigating potential new markets. In some instances they indulge in corporate espionage. This old maxim is still true today, "Always stay close to your family, but get closer to your enemies."

After you have completed these basic steps, you will want to develop a **_Mission Statement_** and that is where we will begin this journey, right after this important introduction to thinking, a prerequisite for understanding this book.

Chapter 1

In the beginning there was thinking and planning
I think, therefore, I am.

As a precursor to all that is to follow, this section is about preplanning. It involves learning the art of thinking. Please read this before you travel on.

Preplanning/Thinking

Before you start planning, start thinking. Visualize what you want to accomplish. See yourself accomplishing it in your mind. Think through the entire process. Be aware that daydreaming is aimless mind wandering whereas thinking is focused concentration. Most of us spend our days daydreaming or processing information instead of thinking.

Much like a computer processes information, our lives are spent mostly doing the same thing, processing. You may say, "Well I think all the time. I talk to myself constantly, therefore I am thinking." Sorry, but that's exactly what you said it is, talking to yourself. Take a look at an average day in the minds of people.

Considering your average day, you wake up, take a shower, dress, eat breakfast and read the paper, check your email or watch the morning news on TV. The next series of actions is concerned with getting to work. However you get to work, bus, train, helicopter, drive yourself, primarily only data processing is involved. You arrive at work and begin the day's tasks.

So far, you have done no real thinking. Driving to work is almost purely automatic and requires only data processing. Most of us talk to ourselves as we drive to work, going over what we have to do that day. That is information processing.

Reading the newspaper and eating are routine processing tasks requiring only minimal attention. Depending on your career, your work will probably require the first thinking you will do today. Also, depending on what it is you do, will dictate, largely, whether thinking is required at all. Many jobs are routine and simply require information processing and reacting to stimuli.

This is not a put down on your job, but merely an exposition that most jobs don't require much thinking, so we learn not to think. An interesting point about this: jobs requiring large amounts of thinking pay more than those that do not. Look around at the different levels of employees in your company. Non-thinkers work harder and receive less income than thinkers who do not work so hard physically but receive much more remuneration.

If you have done little thinking in the past, you may have trouble when you first try. Thinking requires concentration and focusing. To get into thinking, concentration and focusing, practice on some simple subjects. First, select a place with a quiet atmosphere. Sit in a chair and relax, but don't slouch. Close your eyes.

Silently communicate to your body and tell each part to relax starting with your toes and working upward to your brain. Careful! Don't fall asleep. By the way, you are now concentrating and focusing. Remember that activating your mind by thinking requires silence. After all body parts are relaxed, you may want to move deeper into your mind.

An easy way to accomplish this is to count slowly (and silently) to twenty and with each number feel yourself dropping down into your mind. Some people have visual activity seeing themselves slowly moving down a cavern wall eventually reaching a flat surface.

Once the bottom or floor is reached, you start thinking about something you decided to think about before entering the depths of your mind. This is an excellent time to program you, too. Maybe you are not as friendly as you want to be. Tell yourself three or four times, I am a friendly person.

When you finish, you will be semi-conscious so ease yourself into reality by counting backwards from 20 to 0. At 15, pause for a moment and repeat, I am a friendly person. Stop again at five and repeat it once more, except this time, you add, "When I open my eyes, I will be fully awake and have a lot of energy." At zero, open your eyes and you will feel refreshed and ready to pick up where you left off. Do this exercise daily.

Concentration is putting aside all other thoughts and keeping only one thought. Focusing is the narrowing or zeroing in on the subject. Think of a camera as it focuses. You adjust the lens until the subject is sharp, then you push the button.

Remember, the mind is static and requires activity to function; that is thinking. Select some item that you want to accomplish or some small problem you want to solve. A very simple exercise is to choose some object, such as a pencil, and concentrate on it. Keep your eyes closed.

Don't let your mind wander. Visualize the pencil. Observe how it is made. Observe the various parts of the pencil: the lead, the shaved point, the eraser and the metal or plastic clasp that holds it. Notice the color and read the name Ticonderoga No.2. As you do this, the pencil will become sharper in focus and you will see the small dents in the wood made by your teeth when you were unconsciously biting on it.

After you have practiced a bit, try taking on a small goal you want to accomplish. Maybe it's building some shelves in the garage, or a trip you wish to take. Maybe it is correcting some physical problem such as an arthritic finger. Visualize the steps you have to take and see the finished project.

Concentrate on each step as you bring them into sharp focus. Work through the entire project keeping your focus and concentration. See the finished results of your goal. Yes, people have actually cured diseases and other physical problems by concentrating on them and thinking they will be corrected. Now you are thinking, too. Practice and find out what great things you can accomplish. Think big!

Thinking causes an interesting phenomenon. When we begin to think and create things in our minds, thinking becomes the cause in a cause and effect scenario. You have heard the term, "self-fulfilling prophecy." The old joke went like this: I said, "Things could be worse, and sure enough, things got worse." That's because something in the laws of nature picks up the vibrations of positive or negative impulses and brings them into being.

Notice how all the news during 2008 was bad news and sure enough things got worse. Think back to some event in your life where you just knew it wasn't going to happen, you were not going to get what you wanted or you were going to be short of money for a bill. How often did that come true? Ever worried about losing a job? Happened, didn't it?

Well, it works the other way, too. Thinking positive thoughts creates positive results. That is not to say you can cure all ills, or ignore the fact you lost your job and the world is in a recession, but you can look at the positive sides and there always are positive sides.

A simple example is rain. When it rains, we often complain that it is raining. Why? Because it means we will have to wash our car again. You don't have an umbrella and you will get wet. But, look at it from the positive side. The temperature cooled with the rain. Your lawn received a free watering. Your house got a bath.

All the little animals, birds, squirrels, bugs and butterflies are no longer thirsty. All your trees and shrubs were watered, the dust is gone and the streets are clean.

Back to cause and effect. Simply stated, for every effect there is a cause. If you have a problem with a co-worker find the cause, change it and very likely the problem (effect) will go away.

Thinking is causative. Every war started with the thought of war. Every great discovery or invention began with a single thought. Over time, with the thought process working, and the vibrations moving into the universe, a mystical alignment of similar thoughts comes together and eventually something happens; an effect.

It can also be called a manifestation. It can happen quickly or take many years. Consider the submarine and the airplane. Man thought about these for centuries before the manifestation happened. But everything that exists in the outer world was at one time a thought in someone's inner world.

Thinking also brings people together. Have you ever needed help on some idea and almost out of the blue you met someone who was the perfect person to help you? We say it was uncanny. Was it? Or was it simply cause and effect?

Our thoughts and actions have brought us to where we are today. Look back into your past and see for yourself how many good and bad events in your life were results of your thinking and ultimately the outwardly expression of your thoughts – your actions.

Have you ever silently held resentment toward someone? Even though you never said anything there was a barrier between the two of you be-cause you were focused on the resentment and you concentrated on it. If you changed the negative thinking (cause) you became friends with that person (effect). That's where the philosophical statement came from that says the best way to get rid of an enemy is to make a friend of him.

Change the cause and that changes the effect, and that begins with changing your thinking or, in some cases, the other person's thinking. In public relations, this procedure is called behavior modification and you can use it in your business. It is a three-pronged concept.

The first prong in behavior modification is to get others to do some-thing. To do that you must get them to change their behavior and to do that they must first change their attitude. If a person does not buy your

brand, there is a reason. Discover what it is and give that person a better reason to use your brand. Once that is accomplished, you continue
to encourage the new attitude and the action will follow.

Prong 2 is for existing customers. They are already doing what you
want them to do so your goal is to have them continue doing what they
are already doing. Many things from advertising, to incentives, to
listening to them and responding accordingly, accomplish this.

Prong 3 is to allow you to continue doing something you are already
doing. This could involve a new city ordinance that would inhibit your
signage. Here, you might enlist the support of your customers and
march on City Hall.

Now, what has all this thinking stuff have to do with running a business? Everything. You need to understand thinking because this book
requires you to think. It's not a long book and very limited in long ex-
planations and illustrations.

To create a marketing plan that works requires in-depth thinking. It requires visualizing the future you wish to design and developing a way
to make that future happen. Good, positive thinking will carry you a
long way and let you spend restful nights sleeping rather than tossing
and turning or walking the floor. It will put money in the bank and food
on the table. It will free you from worry. It can make you a success.

A final point on thinking: IT'S FREE!

"Most entrepreneurs go into business because they have a passion for their work. The problem is that passion in only half of the equation. Everything else from creating a vision and marketing to project research and analysis in in this book. Since using LaNier's "Make Your Business Sizzle", my sales have doubled in a little less than one month. Yours can too.

Sheilah T. Davis
http://www.ManifestChange.com

Chapter 2

Mission and Vision Statements

Tons of philosophical BS about developing mission statements and thousands of meaningless mission statements exist in businesses everywhere. Consultants make millions by conducting two and three-day séances to construct what is otherwise a worthless piece of hyperbole.

Start by thinking about the two words and what each means, Mission and Statement. Say it another way: What is our reason for being? What are we up to? Is this trip necessary? It is all about why you started the business and what you want to accomplish with it.

Furthermore, your mission statement is nobody's business except yours. Do not hang it up on a big sign at your front door. That is tacky. Do not print it on the reverse side of your business cards either.

IT IS NOBODY'S BUSINESS! More importantly, NOBODY CARES! Also, having a blank side on the card gives you something to write on if you need to jot down important phone numbers or email addresses.

If you have employees, get them involved in the mission statement development process so everyone has a hand in developing your statement. It's much easier to buy into something if you helped create it rather than someone handing it to you and telling you, "This is our mission statement, read it."

If your company is living your mission statement, people will see it in action and that is precisely the best way for them to see it. If not, you surely do not want someone pointing it out on your business card that you are not living up to your own standards.

Revisit your statement every year. Things change and so will your overall mission.

Next, you need to create your *Vision Statement*.

Creating a vision for the future

A vision statement is also for internal use only. Let's start this discussion with a little different definition of vision:

> *We can all see what already exists in the objective world, but what we visualize already exists in the spiritual world, and the visualization is a substantial token of what will one day appear in the objective world, if we are faithful to our ideal... this process of thinking forms impressions on the mind, and those impressions in turn form concepts and ideals and they are in turn the plans...that will weave the future.*
>
> *Charles F. Hannel*

I never use the word foresee for one reason, there is no way to see the future. We can imagine and visualize how we want the future to be and that's what this vision statement thing is all about: visualizing, dreaming, creating something in your mind (inside world) that will someday manifest itself in the outside world, if you are true to your purpose.

We can create a vision for the future and that vision becomes a goal and the goal is attained down line. You cannot foresee that culminating event when you have achieved your goal but you can visualize it and make it happen the way you see it in your mind.

So, dream a little. Be creative about tomorrow, next year. See the success you want and write it down. That's your vision statement. No BS. Real visualization.

Now that we have researched the market, learned to think, and created our mission and vision statements, we are ready to move on to the next level – Planning.

Chapter 3

Planning and Strategy

People's eyes glaze over when they hear the word strategy. It conjures up hours of work and planning. In fact, we all strategize most of the time. Things as simple as driving to work require a strategy: how am I going to get to work? Which streets do I use? I have to beat the7: 30 freight train that always stops traffic for three to four minutes.

Which coffee shop will I patronize and how much money should I withdraw from the bank for the day? All this requires strategy, but we do it automatically in our heads and never really consider that we are creating strategies on the run.

Begin by developing a plan. The first step involves deciding who you want for customers. Let us start by describing your ideal customer from a demographic approach.

A simple way to use demographics is to use the income level of your ideal customer. Just match the costs of your products to the income level required to afford the product and you will know at what economic level your ideal customer must be. (See chapter 5)

Now, you have part of your demographic target. In some cases marital status, gender, number of children, education, make of car they drive and the house they live in could be important. If you sell cars, it helps to know if the prospect owns the make you sell or another brand.

Just make sure you describe your ideal customer completely. Remember, it is not the customers you have now, but the customers you desire to have, so design the ideal customer as close to perfect as you can.

Is that enough? No. We must now move to another area of study called psychographics or lifestyles. This is where the difference in targets shows up.

Lifestyle is usually more important than demographics when determining customers for products.

To understand the difference between demographics and lifestyle, let us take two houses in Middleville, USA that are demographically identical. We will use the example of 45-55 year olds with virtually identical educational and income levels. However, as we look at the lifestyles of each of the two families, the picture starts to change.

House number one: Jim is a Librarian and loves to collect rare books. He spends nearly every weekend in search of these treasures. His wife, May is a teacher and is seriously into gardening. Julie, their oldest child, is a straight A student and uses most of her time practicing the violin. David, her younger brother, fritters away most of his time surfing the Internet.

Next door at house number 2, Paul is an architect. (Remember that these two families are identical from a demographic perspective.) His weekends are spent climbing small mountains and exploring caves.

Arlene, his wife, is an attorney and on weekends, she joins her friends skydiving. Their daughter Sheila, is in her second year of college and their son Artie, is in his last year of high school and plays on the school's football and baseball teams.

Now, when we look at these two demographically identical families from a lifestyle standpoint we get a very different picture. Lifestyles tell us what people do and often why they do it. By using both demographics and psychographics, we can accurately target our customers or potential customers. We can also draft a better message and make a better offer. Additionally, this is essential information for purchasing the proper advertising venues.

Now, let us take this one step further. Suppose you research the area and find there are seventy-five thousand people that fit into your overall criteria. Are you going to try to reach all seventy-five thousand? That could cost a bundle. Why not go back to the drawing board, readjust your income level, and choose the 2 to 3%.

These are people earning enough money to afford your product. Concentrate your mailings, phone calls, ads, whatever you choose to promote your product on this one small group with the highest income. Be relentless in your solicitations. It will pay big dividends.

You may make a few attempts to reach people in the lower income levels, but concentrate on the top two or three percent. When you do this you can approach people saying, we know you are a person who wants quality and can afford it. That is why we want you to be our customer because we provide the highest quality, etc.

Chapter 4

Assets inventory

At this point, let us move to what we call inventory of assets. If you sell products, they are your assets. If you sell a vacation destination the activities, hotel rooms, dining room, and bar are your assets. Whatever adds to your bottom line is an asset.

Determine what type of demographics and lifestyles match your assets. Older people may love easy walking, larger cars, condos with lots of safety devices while younger people have different tastes in food, clothes and shelter. Whatever assets you have, match them to a profile. You create the profile for each asset.

Maybe you sell SCUBA equipment. Your ideal customer is someone who likes water activity, probably owns a boat, and has enough money to afford SCUBA gear and all the paraphernalia that goes with that activity. You may also be interested in including the spouse and any children for a more extended customer profile. Put down everything you can think of that may be of interest to your ideal customer.

Most importantly make sure you match income to your selling costs. If they can't afford it, they won't buy it.

"Whether you're a neophyte business owner or a seasoned pro, this book can dramatically improve your chances to compete and succeed in any market".

Key Howard
Author of An Actor's Life For Me

Chapter 5

Geographics

We have this great big round blue ball floating in space called earth. The big blue marble. Somewhere on earth are the geographical areas where you want to sell your products or services. It may be global or it may be a few square city blocks.

You can select your areas of concentration in a number of ways: throw darts at a map, play spin the globe; just about anyway you want to do it. More than likely you will use group think and select those areas you believe will provide the best results from your marketing efforts.

In many cases this is going to be gut feeling rather than decisions based on research. If you can afford research, that is always the best route to travel. You may already have a history of customers and where they come from.

You will want to add some new ones. One hotelier, who operates an ocean front hotel, said he did his research by walking parking lots of hotels and counting license plates from various states and counties. That gave him an idea where folks were coming from, though not too scientific. Whatever your method, you are going to select from the earth several places that will become your target markets.

For starters, let's say you choose North America. Zero in more. Next, you choose the United States and then Canada. Now, you have two target markets, one being an international market. However, the geography is pretty vast, so let us get more focused.

Let's pick states and provinces. For examples, let's take Pennsylvania, New York, Ohio and Georgia. In Canada, let's just start with Ontario. We may move to Quebec later, but we must remember they speak French so we'll need translations. Let's wait on that move.

Now we have a more manageable list of geographic areas. So, are we finished? Hardly. We must now select the cities within those states; we do this because your advertising world relates to metro areas. That's why you would use Billings, Montana rather than Zortman, Montana. Yeah, there's a place called Zortman. It right close to Lodgepole. Lodgepole? That's in the southeast sector of the Fort Belknap Indian Reservation.

This activity helps you when deciding where to place advertising. No need to advertise to people who live so far away they will never buy from you, unless you are selling on the Internet. If you are, add the Internet as part of your geographical area. Its name is Cyberspace. This is where Facebook, Twitter, You Tube, Linkedin and others come into play.

When you finish selecting the cities in your target markets, you will have a roadmap for selecting the proper media. Remember to use the other two items, demographics and psychographics when researching your media. A final step in this process of demographic, psychographic and geographic profiling is to determine the message you send to potential customers.

We have determined our markets, targeted our potential customers and matched them with our assets. Now we must determine what message to send them. Please understand that this is not an ad copywriting session; it is pure and simple deciding what you want to tell these different groups of people. Your message.

This exercise works much better with several people in your company taking part. Let everyone write a message for every profile and every product or service. You will get many ideas, which is the reason for doing this.

Take each of your groups and decide what you would tell each person if you were talking face-to-face. You want to convince people to do business with you, buy your product and return later to make another purchase.

What would you say to each person on your profile list, if you had one opportunity to convince that person to do businesses with your company? That is your message.

Write your messages under each group heading. Several messages are O.K. Example: We have a family friendly area. It is safe. We are affordable. No other place like it. Our product is made of genuine plastic.

Don't write an epistle. Just put down what you would want to tell your prospective customer. Get as many people involved in this exercise as you wish.

When you finish, have everything typed and organized under group headings: Teens, Boomers, Seniors etc. Next, give this information to your copywriters and they will have great fodder for ad and brochure copy.

Chapter 6

Setting goals

Now it is time for goal setting. Set at least three goals you want to accomplish in a year. Start each goal with the word "To" and make each goal quantifiable and qualifiable. EXAMPLE: To increase revenues 30% by February next year. Notice a goal does not address how you are going to do it. That comes next. A goal is a statement of total commitment.

Do your goal setting carefully. All too often, businesses set goals in haste as though it is something that just has to be done, but it is not important. Actually, it is most important! When the time comes to do this exercise, meet with as many people as you can to get plenty of input. Get ten or twenty potential goals and then decide on the top three. O.K., four if you must, but remember, goals drive your company's sales.

Once you set a goal, immediately under it write the objectives you must accomplish to reach that goal. Each objective is a stepping-stone to the goal. An objective spells out an activity you will use to generate one step toward the goal.

An example of an objective: To develop better relationships with our customers through more frequent contact. Again, much like a goal, it is a statement of commitment and does not describe how it will be done. It is one step out of several.

Finally, under each objective, write a short scenario about how you plan to accomplish that objective. This is labeled, Strategy.

Strategy example: Each month someone from our company will call our customers and ask them a series of questions about how they like our service, our products, our pricing and our employees. In turn, we will give those customers who give us feedback a 25% discount on any item in the store.

Notice how the strategy tells you how you are going to do it; the objective tells you what you are going to do and the goal states what you want to accomplish. And what better way can you accomplish this first goal than to get customers to spend more money, even with a discount.

Once you have achieved a goal, you will probably discover that it then becomes an objective toward an even larger goal. A good example is going to college. When you graduate, you have reached your goal, but if you decide to go to graduate school, graduating from college now becomes an objective toward a new goal, an MBA. .

A final step in goal setting is probably the most important step. You can use this with your business goals and your personal goals. Personal goals? There's a difference? You betcha! You need personal goals to grow, to learn, to accomplish. Much like a business, your personal goals need to be set the same way, quantifiable and qualifiable.

Let's say you want a new car. Your goal then is: To own a new car by June of next year. Next, you state the objectives: To visit dealers in two counties to determine the one I trust most. Third, the strategy: After studying the dealers and determining the price range and the actual car I want I will start negotiating with a salesman.

See? Same way you did the business goals. Any change you want in your life is a subject for goal setting. Now, let's move to that most important step.

Each day, every day, you must do something positive toward your goal. It can be something as small as looking up the address of a car dealer, deciding to set the actual amount of revenue you will need each month to attain your business goal.

This step is the most important step and cannot be over emphasized. One small step a day will bring you closer to your goal. Without the one small daily step, you will have a tendency to forget your goals or ignore them. Ever so often you will run across them and be reminded that you set a goal but you have not done anything to get there. At the end of the year when you do your annual planning you will see that you missed most of your goals and wonder why.

Remove the why from the equation and replace it with One Daily Step. It will automatically keep you goal oriented – guaranteed.

Now you are ready to roll.

Chapter 7

Branding Yourself and Your Business

Branding is probably the most overused word and under used strategy in business today. Large companies spend millions doing it, but small businesses shrug it off as so much nonsense. No wonder why there are so many business failures among small businesses.

If you want to get ahead of the pack, pay attention to your branding.

Branding? Yes, even small businesses need to be aware of branding. Your brand is how people feel about you, how they see you, how they identify you. Make up your mind now how you want to brand yourself and your company before others do it for you. If you don't they will.

Understand, too that a brand exists only in a person's mind. What you buy is the product, but you buy it because the brand is dominant in your mind over all other brands in the same category. This is where the term "Mind Share" originated. A Logo is not the brand; it is a symbol of the brand and used to remind you of the brand and its products.

How do you brand yourself or your company? Many ways. It is the way you dress, the way you answer the phone, your treatment of vendors, customers, anyone who interacts with your business. It is how you use email (do you make corrections, or send out misspelled words in half sentences?) It is the look of your ads, your brochures, any printed material.

Letting the newspaper or magazine create your ads is stupid. Sure, it's cheap (not free; it's included in the ad price). A good ad and a cheap ad very seldom have much in common. Brochures printed on a copier tell me one thing about a business – CHEAP. If your promotional material is cheap, perhaps the quality of your product or service is, too. Many will pass on it.

MAJOR BRANDING ITEM: Remember to follow up. Not doing this causes the loss of more business for the company that fails to follow up and makes more money for the ones that do.

Business cards need only your name, telephone numbers, address, name of the company, web address, email and logo. UNLESS YOU ARE A MODEL, NOBODY CARES WHAT YOU LOOK LIKE! You don't need one of those phony $500 makeover photos on your card that shouts VANITY and EGO.

Do not try to put all your products on your card. A card is simply contact information. It is not a billboard. And don't make the double mistake of using fold over cards.

To begin with, they cost more, they don't fit well in card files and most people don't read all that stuff anyway. They primarily want the contact information. So, give them what they want, not what you want them to have. **A business card is for information; it is not a sales piece. That is the purpose of brochures.**

And, the last word here on branding is Product or Service. It doesn't matter how well you play the branding game, if your product or service sucks, your brand will, too.

Pay particular attention to your branding. It can make or break you.

Chapter 8

Promoting Yourself and Your Company

When you own your own business, you cannot be shy. Promoting your company and yourself is something you must do on a daily basis. In the world of business, "Out of Sight – Out of Mind" is a virtual truism.

Promotion is the best-known P of the Four Ps of marketing. The other three are Product, Price and Place. Promotion includes advertising and public relations. If you don't know what you are doing, you can spend a fortune on advertising and have nothing to show for it except some paid media bills.

Look at your local newspaper. You will see thousands of wasted dollars in ads placed there by small business owners who deal strictly with newspaper reps and don't have any idea what they are doing.

They think they do because the reps have a way of making them believe they know what's best for their business. If those reps are so savvy in running a business, why are they selling ad space?

Not to be kicking reps, we have to have them to place ads, but if you are going to advertise using newspapers or magazines, get a professional to put your ad together. Ad production prices run all over the board. Keep in mind changes and alterations by the client can drive the cost through the roof.

An average ad can run between $350 upwards to thousands of dollars, depending on the complexity and the nature of the content. Photographers and models increase costs tremendously, but amateur models and photographers can reduce the effectiveness of the ad even more, and through inefficiencies, can drive the price up as high or higher as using pros on the job.

How to save on ads.

A few ad agencies resell successful ads created for other clients and tweaked to work for a different business. Transitioning an ad is not difficult and assures the purchaser that the ad has worked previously. While there is no guarantee the ad will work for another business, it has a much better chance than a newly created, untested ad.

Most small business test their ads by actually placing them and hoping they will work. The repurposed ads sell at greatly reduced rates, have run, and have worked. So, why reinvent the wheel? Find someone who knows how to transition proven ads. Most important of all, make sure a professional copywriter writes the copy.

Brochures and other collateral material.

The same goes here. You want the best. Here again, some ad agencies do with collateral material what they do with ads. Moreover, you can save thousands of dollars on artwork because the material you purchase is already finished. It only needs a few tweaks like changing names; photos, logos, copy, and other minor changes, and you have a winner for very little money.

Please note that you will often hear there is too much copy in the ad, brochure or news release. The reasoning is that people don't take the time to read ads with long copy. When you hear that, ask this question:

Why are they looking at a magazine if they don't want to read? It is a well-established fact, based on empirical research, that people do read ads with lots of copy, if they are interested in the product. Let's face it, males seldom, if ever, read ads for feminine products, because they are not interested. But, their wives do.

When it comes to public relations, it is always best to hire a professional copywriter. It will cost you somewhere around $50 to $500 for this strategy.

First, send out periodic news releases to the local media about your business. This is about new products, expansion, new hires, and things like that. Don't use any superlatives or strong adjectives. Second, if your business lends itself to a white paper of some kind, such as a survey or a study, use a good copywriter to produce it.

Newspapers love things like that. It helps you because it casts you in the light of an industry expert. If you have a website, post it on a blog for download. Announce it on your Facebook page. Send Tweets on Twitter. Make a short video and place it on You Tube.

Send an email to all of your customers and prospects. Invite them to visit your blog and download the paper along with a 30% discount coupon they can redeem when they next purchase something from you. Don't worry about writing the article.

That's why you hire the copywriter. Just make sure up front, the writer knows how to do research. Your Webmaster can take care of the rest.

Another item found to be a very effective promotion tool is the business card CD. These small CDs can hold up to 5 or 6 minutes of video. Using video allows you to tell your story eyeball to eyeball with probable purchasers.

Your cost is all up front because the second time you order CDs, you have no production costs on the video portion, unless you want to make some changes. Even with a few changes, you don't incur any large bills.

For budgeting purposes, allocate no more than $8,000 to $10,000. That figure is anticipating using professional people to write, shoot, edit, and burn the CDs.

Shooting with a mini-cam or a flip camera can save the cost of a camera crew. With professional editing, they can look good, but if you want to be sure, go pro.

Just because you get cute shots of your kids and pets does not certify you as a pro on the loose with a mini cam. Some real disasters happen with mini cams because someone tried to save a bundle doing it himself.

Small CDs are terrific handouts at trade shows, networking events and anywhere you run into someone who could become a customer. They come in plastic sleeves and your regular business card slides right inside. A neat package.

The final benefit is the increase of traffic to your web site, because at the end of the video a button appears and a sign that says CLICK HERE TO VISIT OUR WEBSITE. The viewer's hand is already on the mouse....

A very practical book, full of no-nonsense good helpful ideas for any business owner looking to make good use of their marketing budgets."

Fernando Rio
Daytona Referrals

Chapter 9

Networking and Joining Organizations

Two of the best ways to ratchet up a business are networking and joining organizations. Networking costs very little and joining organizations usually requires annual dues of only two or three hundred dollars.

One good business deal can provide a healthy return on your investment. Chambers of commerce, social clubs, athletic clubs, civic clubs and organizations such as the United Way, Easter Seals or the American Cancer Society can be excellent sources of networking and at the same time allow you to give back to your community.

Join any of these organizations only with the thought of what you can give instead of what you can get.

Networking is another one of those overused words. Even party invitations now use freely the word *networking*. However, many people who think they are great net workers have no idea what networking is all about. They see it as a quick turkey shoot in hopes of getting some new business.

You see them at chamber after hours functions: mouth full of food, slopping down a free beer and trying to tell someone how wonderful they are and how they can solve all the other person's problems. They seldom shut up long enough to find out any pertinent information about the other person.

They shove a card at you, ask for yours and dart off to the next food table, leaving you to wipe the food particles off your glasses.

Let us consider the word, network. It probably comes from the fishing industry where nets have been a key tool since man learned to fish. A net is a bunch of holes tied together with a common thread. If you look at the hole and place faces in them, these are the people in your network. Using networking as a net, you can understand the business of networking much better.

Networking, working with a net, is today best symbolized by the World Wide Web. A net is a web. It consists of interconnected units all working together for the good of the whole entity. This is known as synergy and synergy is what you are seeking.

When you seriously begin networking, you will begin by establishing the criteria each member must posses. It's your network and you set the rules. Don't tell people that you are putting them into your network. It is not an organization with dues and meetings – it is your network. By not telling people they are in, they never know if you drop them out, which occasionally you will do. Besides, they may not want to be in your network.

As you meet people, no matter where, get to know them. An initial meeting is not a sales call; it is a discovery session. You want to discover as much about the person as you can without seeming too overbearing or intrusive. You must learn the art of asking questions without crossing the line to prying.

VERY IMPORTANT: Some members of your network will never bring you any business. A very good reason why you need a large network. The reason you want to ask questions is to enable you to decide if you want that person in your network. Over time, you will construct a network of people who meet your network criteria.

My network stretches from Hong Kong and Cambodia across the United States and Canada to the United Kingdom, Germany, Sweden, The Netherlands and France. I have been building this network for 38 years, even before computers. I have removed many people for many reasons, Some have disappeared, some have died. Most have never given me any business or referred me, but they are friends and we correspond regularly.

I keep the list on my email in a special network folder. I also have a backup on disk and a printed copy in my safe. I consider this list as part of my working capital. Why do I keep people on the list who do not send business my way? Simple. Each has a special place. I have about fifteen people to whom

I send ads, brochures, articles and anything I am producing for clients. Why do I do that? They are my online focus group. They are honest with me and don't sugar coat their responses. They often point out things I have overlooked. That is a valuable resource for my clients and me.

I sometimes collaborate with members when writing articles and books. A case in point: I have known a lady in Birmingham, Alabama since 1971. She was a writer for a national magazine when I met her. She retired as a senior editor of that magazine. During those years, I never once received a line of copy in any of her publications. She was always writing about things I was not involved with. Nevertheless, we stayed in touch.

Over the years, I saw her two or three times at trade shows, we talked on the phone once in awhile, and emailed regularly when email arrived on the scene. Now that she is retired, she is writing things she wants to write about and we are considering working on a book together. It took 38 years but it looks as though we may finally do something together – and we have been friends for a long time.

On the fun side, I have one network member in Germany who purchases food items for me that are not available in the United States. I have her bank account number, and she always is reimbursed immediately.

Actually I use another network member who lives in the same city as she does, but has a bank account here where I live. I put the money into his account locally and email him when it is done. Then he makes a local deposit in Germany into her bank account. Another great use of networking.

I have never told anyone in my network that they are in my network. Those who network probably know they are and that's OK.

To close out on networking, you can network at meetings designed for networking, but most are parties, so have a good time. Once in awhile, you will luck out and meet someone who is a right fit. Referral organizations may be good for you. That depends on at what level you work in business to business. If it is at the C level, these organizations don't help much. Find one made up of C level people.

Historically the best way to go is to build your own network, nourish it and use every activity you can find to recruit more people to your network. Ultimately, the people in your network will provide the most business for you.

Joining organizations is necessary for anyone in business. To be successful you must be known, and to be known you must be seen. A word of caution: **DO NOT JOIN** any organization just to get known. Get known by the service you render to that organization.

Be an active member or don't be a member at all. Your name on the roster means nothing, and if you don't show, you will appear insincere and your plus becomes a negative.

Don't be a joiner if you can't contribute and get involved. Volunteer, bring in new members and remember to donate as much as you can if it is a charitable organization.

It doesn't matter what organizations you join; they all have networking possibilities. Join those that closely align with your life and your allegiances. You may want also to check out several online network organizations such as Linkedin or one of the social networks such as Facebook or Myspace.

Chapter 10

Financial Control

Three prime reasons businesses fail: Bad management, Lack of controls and Insufficient capital.

Up to this point, you have established your market, where and who it is. You have set goals, objectives, and strategies to reach them. You have identified tools you will use, and now it is time to look at the financial side of the business planning process.

What was your net income in March of last year? The year before? In which month of the year do you have the greatest amount of net income? Ask the same questions about your gross income. You need to know this, so let us move in on to that subject now.

This is an exercise you do every year at the end of your fiscal year. If you do your budgeting a month or two early, you will have to project what you think your income will be in the remaining month or months of your fiscal year. You can correct it later.

This is pre-budget planning and a step many people in small businesses don't even know exists. Yet, to establish a budget, you must first determine how much money you expect to have coming in during the year.

We are going to deal only with your net revenue at this point, the money that you will use to operate your business. So, remember to use net figures. The easiest way to understand net is: the amount of money you have left after you pay suppliers. It is what's left to pay your regular company expenses and salaries.

First, you will set up a page similar to the example shown here. Beside each month, place the amount of net income you received in each month for each year. Total each line, across and down. Next, divide each month's 3-year total by the annual total.

Complete your entire row through December. Now, you have the percentage that each month provides toward the annual net revenue based on an average of the past three years. The figures are rounded to achieve 100%.

The final step is to determine by what percentage factor you want to increase revenues for the coming year. Assuming an 8% goal, take the 2009 total of $591,250 and multiply by 8%. That gives you a figure of $47,300. Add that to the $591,250 and your new goal is $638,550. (Not totally accurate but close).

The final step in this process is to multiply the new goal by each month's percentage and that will tell you what you must achieve monthly to reach your income goal. If the percentages do not equal to the total, redo the calculations until you reach 100%. After the first year, it is much easier to do since all you do is drop off the oldest year, add the newest year's figure, and repeat the process.

FIG.1

	2007	2008	2009	Total	%	Goal
Jan	52,000	47,500	46,250	145,750	7.69	49,104
Feb	56,000	55,250	58,500	169,750	9	57,470
Mar	61,500	63,000	52,250	176,750	9.14	58,363
Apr	77,000	75,000	51,000	203,000	11	70,241
May	68,000	68,500	49,250	154,000	8	51,084
Jun	56,000	49,500	48,500	154,000	8	51,084
Jul	51,250	50,000	48,250	149,500	7.75	49,487
Aug	53,000	49,500	48,250	150,750	8	51,084
Sept	49,000	48,500	46,000	143,500	7.42	47,380
Oct	57,000	47,000	46,250	150,250	8	51,084
Nov	54,500	49,500	49,250	153,250	8	51,084
Dec	53,250	50,500	47,500	151,250	8	51,084
Total	**688,500**	**653,750**	**591,250**	**1,933,500**		**638,550**

If you do this exercise each year, you will always know at a glance, what your income was for the past three years, month by month. It also shows any trends toward cycles, or if the business is starting to wane. It is a great tool for giving you a picture of where you have been and where you are going.

The next exercise is the same except you will use your gross revenue figures instead of net. When you complete this chart, you will have a goal for gross revenue the same as you have for net revenue.

Why do we do two versions? Simple. The gross revenue tells you how much money you must generate to make the net. It is a picture of your sales and fees during the past three years. Now you have a chart that tells you how much sales revenue you need to generate each month to achieve your net. Thus, you have set your sales goal.

Once you have completed that chart, it's time to move to the budgeting process. This is another area that small businesses neglect, which can become a fatal mistake. Here is an easy way to build your budget. It requires some work, but after the first year, it is an easy process.

Use a 13-column sheet for this exercise. You can get books of these at any office supply store. To begin, list the name of every cost item you have in your business, such as rent, telephone, electricity, insurance, Social Security and Medicare matching, salaries, etc.

Be sure to list all insurances. Let's say that you pay auto insurance twice a year. Take the total amount and divide by 12. This gives you a monthly amount to budget. Each month move that amount to a savings account so it can accumulate and earn interest at the same time.

After you have every item you can think of listed, you may want to rearrange them into some order. For example, list advertising, public relations, sales promotion and trade shows under the heading of Marketing; salaries, medical insurance, 401K, SS and Medicare under administrative and so on.

If you want to really get into this, talk to your accountant and use a numbering system so you have line item numbers. You can get by without them but they are useful as you grow, and your accountant will love you.

Next, using historical data, estimate the annual figure for each item. Then divide by twelve and that will put you in the ballpark. Salaries will vary, so try to estimate start of the year and then include any raises. Any line item that is apt to change during the year needs to be manually adjusted for those changes. You may not know when the changes will occur, but make an educated guess. When they do occur, make the adjustment.

When you have all of your annual figures, place those at the far end of the sheet and label that column TOTAL. Next, label the twelve remaining columns by months, starting with the first month of your fiscal year.

After you have everything labeled, enter the amount of money budgeted for each item by month. When you finish, each column should tally up to the amount under Total. Then, add each monthly column from top to bottom and enter that total at the bottom of the sheet. Next, add the monthly totals across and the figure you get should be the same as the figure already under the total column.

Now, go back to the first chart where we used net figures and compare your estimated income goal with the total you just developed in your budget. If your budget is smaller than your estimated income goal, you win. If it is larger, you have two choices: cut the budget or figure a way to earn more money.

Either way, you have developed a powerful economic tool for managing the finances of your company. Now, one more exercise, the ultimate control mechanism.

Using the same 13 column sheets, set up your budgeted items (line items) the same way as before. This time however, use three columns for each month. Label the first column Budget, the second Actual, and the third Variance. Place the name of the first Month over the three columns.

Continue until you have twelve months. This will require more than one sheet. In the first column, enter the budgeted amount for that month. Continue through the twelve months. These are the identical numbers you have on the master budget. Go through each item the same way.

When you finish, you have a control sheet in front of you. Each month, enter the exact amount you spend for each item in the Actual column. Subtract that amount from the budgeted amount and enter the number in the Variance column. If you spent less you will have a positive variance.

If you spent too much, you will have a negative variance. Put those figures in (brackets) to show negative amounts. If you were right on the money, just place a short line – to indicate no variance. Do that each month and you will learn quickly how to manage your money and never run out of cash.

Chapter 11

Putting it all together

Here is where you assemble all the parts to achieve SYNERGY. This is also, where many small business owners refuse to go, and thereby forfeit the benefits this next section offers.

Actually, at this point, if you have done all he things you were asked to do, you are pretty close to having a workable marketing plan. Remember, we talked about promotion? That includes advertising, public relations and sales promotion. Now is the time to decide what you are going to do for the coming year.

You have established a budget and if you can afford it, you have an advertising line item. What you must do now is decide where you will spend the money. TV? Radio? Print? Out of doors? Internet? So many media, so little money. Look at your market and your customers. Revisit the ideal customer profile.

What do they read, listen to or watch?
Do take care about on line advertising. It may be OK for companies with large budgets but if your budget is small it may not be your best avenue. However, with a good web site and proper promotion of the site, you can mix it up just like the big guys do.

When you decide which medium or media you will use, do the research. Most of it is on line. Use Google or Dogpile and find what you are looking for. Get the rate cards. Study them and decide how you will place your advertising. Make a schedule for each month. Use a spreadsheet or use the old 13-column sheet you used for your budget.

At this stage, you are playing with figures. Don't worry about ad design, just how much money you will spend to place your advertising. Show each medium on a separate line. This way, you will always know how much is going for newspaper and how much is going for radio, etc.

When you are finished with the advertising schedule, do the same thing for public relations. Schedule news releases, articles, trade shows, and the production of collateral material such as brochures, posters, the business card CDs and anything else you plan to produce to help your sales effort.

Trade shows can be beneficial or disastrous. Pick and choose carefully. If you can't afford to be in a show, attend anyway. Often you will find you can still do a bit of business or networking simply by being there and walking around. Be creative.

Sales promotion activities need to be scheduled and budgeted. If you are a financial planner or an attorney involved in helping people with retirement planning, you may schedule several luncheons or dinners throughout the year to bring potential customers together for a presentation. That's sales promotion.

If you own a candy store and you periodically give free samples, that's sales promotion. Schedule it and keep track of the cost because that comes under the cost of doing business.

With the completion of the promotion scheduling, you now have a simple, workable marketing plan. If money is tight, be resourceful and beef up the activities that don't cost much, especially the public relations activities.

By scheduling all activities, you know where you are going and how you will get there. The main thing to remember is to be creative in all you do and never give up, never give up.

Your marketing plan has all the goals you plan to achieve. You have your sales goals, your revenue goals and a budget, all based on historical data generated by you. You also have control mechanisms in place to help manage your money. One step to go.

Chapter 12

Controlling your business

Controlling your business is not always easy. Not controlling it is a quick way to bankruptcy.

When you have everything assembled take this last step and add in a module that will keep your plans current and on track.

First, plan several times a year to assess your situation. Conduct a situation analysis. Where are we today? Where are we supposed to be? If you are on track, GREAT! If not, why? What happened? How can we correct it?

Second, conduct a four-step process to fine-tune your plans. See Fig.2

Step 1 – Research. Use the Four Ts. Talk To The Target. You know who the target is, it is your customer or a probable purchaser. Ask questions. How are we doing? What products do we not provide that you would purchase if we did. How is our service? How can we make it better? You can make up more, but ask them, then...Listen. Hear what they are saying.

Write down their responses and read them later. Repeat this process with every customer you can. Remember to listen and hear. Do not argue, do not discuss, just listen and ask more questions. Then, go back to your desk and study the results.

If you are adept at the computer, consider using one of the online survey companies to survey your customers and prospects. You get good results and it creates a great image of your business.

Step 2 – Planning. Yep, more planning. Use the information you gained from your analysis and from your customers to tweak your existing plans. Delete anything that is not working. Change where change is required and install new things if needed. Do not be afraid to drop things that are not working, even if you like them. Never fall in love with your business or your programs. Continue to use only those elements that work.

Step 3 – Implementation. Now, get back to work and put into action the new items in your plan.

Step 4 – Analysis. In three to six months, repeat steps 1 through 3.

FIG.2

RESEARCH

ANALYSIS PLANNING

IMPLEMENTATION

As a bonus for reading this epistle, if you run into a brick wall on your journey to success and feel as though you are hopelessly confused on any point covered in this book, contact me and if I can help you, I will. If I can't, I will tell you and point you in the proper direction. My email address is genelanier@yahoo.com.

Good hunting!